A Bite-Sized Business Book

Fast Restaurant Growth in the New Pandemic Economy

How to Win the New Restaurant On-line Battle for Customers and Profit . . .
Even if You Can't Spell App

Neil Murphy

Published by Bite-Sized Books Ltd 2020
©Neil Murphy 2020

Bite-Sized Books Ltd Cleeve Road, Goring RG8 9BJ UK
information@bite-sizedbooks.com
**Registered in the UK. Company Registration
No: 9395379**

ISBN: 9798678993946

Contents

Introduction

A New World and Opportunity Emerges

Depending on the date you're reading this book, Coronavirus could be a thing of the past and everything is relatively well in your world. Customers are happy to be back, in full swing, visiting your restaurant, pub, takeaway or coffee shop without any concerns for their health, not a face mask to be seen, money flowing out of people's pockets and straight into yours with full abandon. Online technology, mobile phone usage, marketing your business like you used to pre Covid-19, has automatically kicked in and it's like nothing has changed at all. It was all a horrible bad dream that felt like at times it was a never ending, continuing economic and emotional nightmare for many businesses in the food and hospitality sector.

And yet, sorry to wake you but Covid-19 *did* happen, and it's resulting economic impact and ramifications are probably in place in some way, shape or form as you read this book. A second or third wave on the horizon? Who knows. We've got to wait and see. However, what you don't want to do is to twiddle your thumbs and to wait and see what you're going to do about what's happened, and what may still be happening.

If you want to win this game, you can't wait and see and roll up into a ball and play dead and think it'll all go away, hoping, wishing, praying that everything will be back to normal, as it was. And depending on who you listen to for advice, help and information, there are many wise heads telling us life is not going to revert back to normal as we know it, any time soon.

And so what that means for you is there's an interesting opportunity for you to think about that's presenting itself to you through this thunderstorm of chaos and confusion. And that opportunity is to embrace and take advantage of the **new factors** that are in your favour. Specifically, paying real close attention to the title of this admittedly provocatively titled book – **Fast Restaurant Growth in the New Pandemic Economy – How To Win The New Restaurant Online Battle For Customers & Profits… Even If You Can't Spell App!**

Because, if you take to heart what you're about to read in the following pages, you and your restaurant, pub, takeaway, or other food based business can come out of this **Economic Darkness** with a completely new strategy and battle plan to create both immediate cash flow and long-term stability and equity. And that too, without you having to be a technology whizz or an automation wizard. None of that is true, or, necessary.

However, what IS true, and whether you like hearing it or not is not up for debate because the marketplace actually doesn't care what any of us think, is that there is a new world order rearranging itself in the restaurant and hospitality sector, locally, nationally and globally. It's those who are smart, agile

4

and quick to embrace new and different thinking and actions who'll truly prosper.

And no matter if you operate a single unit on the corner of your street or if you have multiple outlets and you're a big name in the industry, or anything in between, if you're suffering economically, if you're devoid of the right and proper information to help you make and educated and intelligent choice in what you're going to do next, and you now want a fresh new perspective laid out for you in simple plain English that'll show you how you can win the restaurant game, no matter what's going on in the Economy, good times or bad, then you'll be finding it hard to sleep at night once you finish reading this book. It'll agitate, prod and provoke you into taking new actions and doing things, differently.

My wish for you is to embrace all you read here and then ask yourself after you've finished reading it... "*maybe...maybe there's something here I need to dig a little deeper into if I want to thrive and win, despite what's gone on in the past*".

Chapter 1

Who This Book Is For?

This book is for restaurant owners, Pub owners, Takeaways, Coffee shop owners who are hurting, yet are now ready, hungry, inspired, seriously committed to making a winning comeback after the economic Covid-19 lockdown disaster, and... the crippling ramifications that have since followed.

This book is for you if you want the right and proper information to help you win the restaurant battle, to be informationally and strategically even stronger than before, where your newfound intentions and drive will render your local competitors as bewildered and insignificant bystanders. It's also for those who are now willing to listen more than they talk, and to now listen with the intention of understanding and absorbing what's working, currently, right now, in this precise moment because who knows if Covid-19 will return in full force.

This publication is for you if you feel you find yourself slipping down a deep and dark hole and don't feel you have the energy and stamina to carry on, where you feel like packing everything in, but... there's that entrepreneurial voice inside you almost dragging you up and out of that dark hole, and where you now know and feel deep in your bones that you're going to turn things around. And that you've already worked way too hard in your business already just to throw in the towel.

This is for you if you're constantly throwing ideas around in your head as to whether or not to open up at all because of the relative costs of staying open doesn't make practical or financial sense, yet you know inside there's got to be a way to make it work yet you're missing that final piece to the complete the puzzle, and you're going to search for it until you find it.

This publication is also for you if you're either in the dark about online technology, mobile Apps and automated ordering and where your mind just belly flops when it's all mentioned. And yet you know there's a voice somewhere inside you that says if you can just get the right and proper information, and it's explained to you in simple ABC language, that you'll be able to win this restaurant game.

And finally, this publication is for you because you're now open and willing to let new ideas and new information flow in because you know that your old systems and old ways of marketing and bringing in customers isn't going to cut it in the new world reality we're all facing. What that means is you're now ready to show up with a beginner's mind and are willing to experiment and test in a way that you wouldn't have necessarily done so before.

Chapter 2

Who This Book Is Definitely NOT For

Frankly, If I had a magic genie and rubbed its tummy and have it grant me my 3 wishes, my first wish would be to have this publication be sent and put in front of all restaurant owners, takeaway owners, pub owners and anyone selling prepared food to customers, who are hurting and who are in some kind of financial bind, and to have this book be their bedside reading, their morning and afternoon reading.

Alas however, not all owners are the same. Not all possess the same willingness and desire to pull themselves up and out of sticky situations. Many like to complain and moan to anyone who'll listen, rather than roll up their sleeves to solve and solutionise.

And so that's why this publication will do you zero good at all if you're looking for quick fix short cuts just to bring in a short burst of cash flow, with no eye on installing the necessary ongoing business and marketing systems that are absolutely needed if you want to bring in dependable, ongoing income in a reliable, systematic and predictable way.

This publication is also definitely not for the restaurant owner, pub or coffee shop owner who thinks there's just no answer to their specific and precise problem, that their business has a unique set of problems and that they can't be solved. And frankly, it's that kind of thinking, and the promotion of it, it's that precise thinking and held-on-to-beliefs that'll cause many more businesses to shut their doors for good.

And finally, this book is definitely not for someone who read, reads, reads and implements next to nothing. The contents of this book has to be devoured and then, a constructive plan, made and followed up on, accordingly. However, if you're unwilling to start the process then there's no-one else to blame, no-one else to complain to, no-one to persuade who'll buy into your story.

You can change all that, if you choose to.

Chapter 3

How Do You Compete and Win When Your Already Razor Thin Margins Are Being Slashed and Eroded to the Bone Even More?

How do you win the online game for local orders when there are third party companies continually feasting on your margins by extracting restaurant commissions and customer transaction fees, how do you win that game?

The global growth of online orders for takeaways has been a fat cash cow for many companies like just eat who have built their brand and revenue through restaurant commissions and transaction fees. And those charges exist even when your loyal customer make repeat orders, and... for as long as they *continue* to make repeat orders.

Let me repeat that once again in case it didn't register or sink in.

There are restaurants, takeaways, coffee shops and pubs who are paying commissions and transaction fees each time a new customer or repeat customer orders or buys food through the services of a third party online ordering App or website. And what that means is a business will be paying commissions and fees for the rest of their life. And to top it all, they'll never actually own those customer's contact info and details.

Now if you've been following along and have been paying careful attention, you'll know at a deep cellular level that the value and equity in your business lies inside the stored value resident in your customers. And yet, if you don't own that customer data and information, you cannot enjoy and bank the money you're continually giving away in fees and commissions to third party online ordering companies.

Restated: you can get 100% of all your own sales of your own customers instead of paying out paying out 14% of it (sometimes up to 25% of it) to middleman App agencies who act like vultures on a feeding frenzy, looking to swoop down on your vulnerabilities. And, who do it with charming insincerity.

However, **if you know the one crucial secret** that'll not only have you be able to take advantage of what the online ordering company can do for you, you can at the same time, enjoy fatter margins and never have to pay another transaction fee or ordering commissions... AND... you can have **complete access to YOUR customer's data** that has been deliberately hidden out of plain sight from you. And I'm going to share that secret with you shortly.

Chapter 4

Where on Earth Did My Customers Go?

How are you going to win the Restaurant game if all your customers decide to put on their socks and shoes and march on out of your business, and... head straight into the loving and welcoming arms of your competitor just down the road from you, what are you going to do, how can you win, if you lose your customers?

The more important question for now is to answer why did they go and march out in the first place, and what can we do to stop that from happening?

But an even deeper question is what did you do, or not do, to make that all happen? And let's be clear, in this new economy that we're slap bang in the middle of, the key to what happens, is all about taking responsibility for our actions and the truth around it all that'll set us free. And personal responsibility and taking the right actions will be the driving factors that'll make the biggest difference in how you're going to come out of this scenario - smiling and happy, or dejected and defeated.

So where did your customers go?

Well, here's an accurate list of *why* customers leave a business:

1% die. There's obviously nothing we can do about that percentage of people but what we can do if we're aware of the fact, is to send a message of regret or condolence to family members if we know who they are.

3% Move. It happens of course. Greener, newer pastures. New challenges. New life circumstances. Now if it happens that they've only moved a few miles or kilometres from where they resided previously, there's an opportunity to send them a 'New Home Eat In Special', or some variation of that.

5% Listen to a Friend's advice and Switch to an alternative vendor. That happens when someone really has had an incredible experience in one place, and decides to tell all they know as a natural and excited consequence of their experience. We all do it. And yet, we do it very infrequently because there really aren't that many exciting experiences to be had. And that's an opportunity there for you to be doing things differently and to be talked about so not only will your customers not want to switch to any other business for the food and service you provide, but also, you'll have a lot more newer customers flooding in to your venue because of what your existing customers tell them.

9% switch because of a better price or product. In a like for like scenario, where everything is pretty much the same as everyone else you're competing against, without any other clear distinction or difference, price will be the key differentiator that'll determine where your customers will go. But, if you want to stop those % of people from switching over to another vendor, then you want to focus on providing a better all round quality product and experience.

14% switch because of being dissatisfied with the product or customer service. Frankly, it doesn't matter how good your service or how high you rank on those areas that'll make the biggest impact and difference to the overall experience of your service and product, there'll be people who'll complain and whine, no matter what. The best thing to do in those instances is to let those customers go and let them haunt someone else's establishment.

Now the way to reduce genuine dissatisfaction is by quickly and courteously responding to, and solving the problem or dissatisfaction a customer has. There's nothing worse for a customer having a legitimate complaint, and not having it quickly acknowledged and acted on. And what happens with an unhappy, dissatisfied customer who is still unhappy and dissatisfied? That's right. They'll tell anyone else who'll listen. And with information being sent and received almost instantly, thanks to the internet and mobile technology, both good and bad news gets to its intended audience at lightning fast speeds. And bad news adds up. 14% could be a lot of lost business for you annually.

Like hearing it or not, the BIGGEST loss of customers to a business is because 68% of customers leave because of feeling uncared for, unappreciated, not acknowledged, not communicated to. Let me say that again:

68% of customers leave a business because of feeling uncared for, unappreciated, not acknowledged, not communicated to.

Most customers don't leave a business because of the technical or service related reasons cited above, illogical as that sounds when you think of hard core business reasons. The simple facts are that just like you, your customers are people with emotions and feelings and sensitivities. And as such, they all want to feel connected, to think that they matter, that they're special in some way.

And just by the simple act of acknowledging that and staying in touch in a continuous and systematic way with your customers, you'll have customers for life. They wouldn't want to go anywhere else. Why would they? They're treated with care and kindness and they feel that you're an integral part of their life. There's no need to go anywhere else.

In an upcoming chapter, I'll share one the of most cost effective and efficient ways you can stay connected and in communication with your customers so that a high % of them will want to stay with you for the long haul, whilst at the same time, have them feed you all the profits, cash flow and new customers you could ever want.

Chapter 5

It's Not the Customers Job to Remember to Come Back, It's Your Job to Remind Them to Come Back.

On the whole, we human beings are fickle and need constant reminding about many things. And unless we're reminded, we don't do what we're supposed to be doing. So we lapse into an automatic habitual behaviour pattern that's not very good for us.

For example: We don't stick to an exercise plan unless we're reminded that we're looking a little portly. We don't pay our taxes on time unless prompted and prodded by the penalty notices coming through the door. We don't take our cars in for servicing unless we get the reminders or we see a brake fluid light or red fuel light brightening up the dashboard. We don't wake up at the time we've planned unless we've set an alarm to do so.

Same is true for your restaurant, pub, coffee shop or takeaway customer. If left to their own process, they'll come in or order when they want. At a time, that's governed and dictated by them.

And yet, with a little careful nudging and programming of those customers, we can not only have them come in and order on a more frequent and regular basis, but we can increase the order value each time they do come in or place an order, thanks to careful bundling and packaging up of higher value meals and additional items.

Many Restaurants, takeaways and pubs have little to no system or plan to remind customers to order a takeaway or book a table who have done so, previously. And yet, that's where the entire wealth and equity inside a business lies – in the stored value of all past and current customers.

Most business owners feel they've done the hard work in acquiring a customer (which by the way, is the most expensive business activity any business undertakes) and so they live and operate by the mantra - *once a buying customer, always a buying customer*. Meaning, they'll come in and buy when they're ready to do so, so we don't need to do anything but wait until they show up.

And yet, customers won't show up in a regular way unless they remember to do so based on their own desires. They need to be triggered into action, more regularly. Because who knows, a local competitor could have shown up, wooed that customer, did a great job in that, and now, continually communicates with them. So because of that forming of a relationship, that customer you thought you had an iron cage around, has now all but gone from your business and into the welcoming arms of the local establishment around the corner.

And that'll all because you thought you've done your job in acquiring that customer and yet, the real value is in the continual communications and in the forming of a relationship with that customer. Anything else is a business plan built on guesswork and hope. And frankly, that's the very operating model of many owners in the local restaurant, food and hospitality business – guesswork and hope. And it's that specific thinking and belief that has, and will continue to, cripple a business, Covid-19 or not.

So what do you do to get your customers coming back in and buying, in a regular and consistent way?

The simple answer is that you communicate. It's not hard to do. And with a variety of inexpensive ways, and available media (text messaging, Facebook, email, even via your own App), it's never been easier to keep in touch and follow up with your customers.

But what do you communicate? And, when?

Now depending what restrictions are currently like for restaurants, pubs, takeaways, cafes, coffee shops, etc…at the time you're reading this, you can't go wrong by announcing a special promotion each calendar month. And when you think about it, there are plenty of events, occasions, celebrations, holidays, taking place each calendar month and all you need to do is build a simple communication to tell your customers about it, via your chosen media format.

For example, here are a few special events you can tie in each month on your promotional calendar:

January   New Year's Eve

February	Valentines
March	Summer time / Clocks go forward / Mother's Day
April	Easter
May	Bank Holidays
June	Wimbledon Tennis / Father's Day
July	World Chocolate Day
August	Summer Holidays
September	Back to School
October	Halloween
November	Guy Fawkes
December	Christmas

And yet, there's probably something going on each week of each month of the year you could tie in to a simple promotion.

Getting in touch and staying in touch has never been this easy, or this cheap. And yet, most businesses still don't do it, still-don't keep in touch. But why not? There are a number of reasons.

They think it's too expensive. Or too complicated. Or too time consuming. Or just not necessary.

And yet, each month the same conversation carries on regardless... that there's a continual struggle to bring in the money, a struggle to pay the bills, a struggle to get the customers in, whereas you've seen, it can all be fixed relatively easily.

Once you make a plan and commitment to implement the simple communications each and every week, you'll transform your business. And later on, in this publication, I'll show you an almost quite unbelievable way where you can run your entire business from the palm of your hand, and still make more money from your restaurant or food business that you might have thought was not at all possible.

The key?

Simple yet effective and powerful follow up carried out in a consistent and efficient way.

Chapter 6

Why Don't Your Customers Complain?

Whenever I ask restaurants, takeaways, pubs, coffee shops and others, if they get many complaints from their customers about anything to do with the business –

Whether if the food was cold or undercooked, if it didn't arrive in time, if payment was too confusing, if the lines were too long, if the phone wasn't answered within a reasonable time frame, if the online process was too clumsy or confusing, if the staff weren't cordial or friendly, or any other number of possible areas of complaint.

Whatever *could* be a problem, most owners almost always pride themselves is saying that on the whole, they don't receive complaints.

And yet, what owners aren't aware of is even if customers aren't complaining, a number of those unhappy customers will silently never ever come back again, thus taking with them their own current purchase value, their on-going residual value, and, their referral value. All of that, gone. And gone to another place or venue who'll get that current customer value and that customer's entire future monetary value.

If you want the clear numbers, whether you know it or not, it's estimated that 96% of unhappy customers don't complain. However, 91% of those who don't complain, won't order online again or visit the venue again.

But the bad news isn't over.

That's because a dissatisfied customer will tell between 7-12 people about their bad experience. And if you can take the economic shock of all that, go back to the chapter to do with Lifetime customer value and you'll see that each customer could be potentially worth over £1000 over 4 years – that's a potential 7k - 12k of business that'll now never come to you because of that single customer who walked on out with their complaint tucked under their arms and that complaint was never brought to the attention of the owner.

Expand that out to more than just one unhappy customer walking out, and to who they'll tell, and that's a potential six figure income stream that'll just float on by your business and you'll never ever come to know why. But now, you *do know* why!

Now here are 5 main reasons people don't complain:

1. It takes so much effort
2. Customers feel there's no point
3. People don't like confrontation
4. They don't want staff fired
5. Business never asked if there were any problems or issues

Receiving customer complaints and solving them fast, is a process you want to run toward and embrace because with that attitude and approach, you'll not only soon have a process to sort and handle all customer complaints in a way that'll have those customers delighted, ecstatic, many not wanting to leave the business at all even if you messed up in a big way. And also, they'll happily tell 7 - 12 other people how majestically you handled their complaints and how because of that, you could generate a ton of new, ongoing referral business that you'll now know how to maximise their lifetime customer value to you and your business.

How can you quickly handle customer complaints?

By getting your customers to tell you about it all.

And how can you get that insight and feedback from your customers – and have it all simplified through a process that's dead easy to put into action?

I'll share that with you shortly.

Chapter 7

The Goldmine in Your Business Is in the Strength of the Customer Relationship

Why is it that one business can have customers in the thousands, but is less profitable than a business with customers in the low hundreds? So, what's going on here?

You could be somewhat mistaken for thinking that it's purely because of the quality of the food and so that's why the business with relatively low numbers of customers can charge way more money, so bulking up the cash flow and profits.

And don't get me wrong, good quality food is part of the winning formula to higher profits. However, there's a more crucial element that'll continue to make the cash tills sing. And that is because of the ongoing quality of relationship a business has with their clients and customers.

Think about this. How frequently would you visit a restaurant if you've no real connection or relationship with the owner and staff? How much of an experience would you have if you simply get your food, eat it, pay your bill and walk out after, without any kind of deep or meaningful interaction?

On the other hand, what kind of relationship do you think is developed when you have the owner welcome you like a long lost friend, wanting to hear about what's happened since they last saw you, who sends you a special message either by text or email ...to thank you personally again for coming in to their business?

Further, what do you think would be the quality of the relationship if you were sent an exciting and compellingly written newsletter, embedded with video links to specific recipes, a conversation with the chef, the owner, staff. A behind the scenes look at what new things are coming your way, a special invitational offer each month to a special event you're being invited to, a birthday card or anniversary message sent by the owner to you... what kind of impact and value do you think this will have on your business if you continue to develop these kind of relationships with your customers?

The answer is obvious; you'll have built a level of goodwill and equity in your business to such a level that it'll ensure your customers remain an integral part of your business for the short, medium and long term. They fund your life.

And don't be surprised to know that even when you suffer some kind of catastrophe or collapse, your customers will remain by your side, ready to help and engage with you because you've already made huge relational and good will deposits in your customers' emotional bank accounts with your communications, your sincerity and your genuine interest in your customers as real human beings that the natural extension of that investment you've made in them is to have that reciprocated in like manner. And they'll only be too happy and thrilled to help. What an exciting business scenario to be part of.

And what about the knock on impact and effect this'll have on your staff? Frankly, when you give anyone a fantastic environment to work in, a place where they're respected and valued, cared for and cherished...well, just try keeping them away from working at your business! You can't. They'll just LOVE working there. They'll love working for... YOU!

And the good thing is that building this kind of relational equity doesn't take a stack of additional money that you have to pour into your business. It doesn't. All it starts with is a shift of mind and a shift towards falling in love with your customers like you do with family and friends. And this is available for any restaurant, takeaway, pub or coffee shop to employ and benefit from, right away. Especially with the low cost, uncomplicated communication tools that are available. And they're also the very channels and methods your customers are currently using and like to be contacted by and communicated to by. I'll talk about this in an upcoming chapter.

If you make forming deep relationships with your customers a continual way of operating your business by, you'll never have a marketing or cash flow problem ever again, no matter which way the economic winds are blowing and no matter what your local competition might be doing. Because strong relationships means your customers will be internally compelled to order or dine in, more often, spend more whilst they're there, and ultimately and effortlessly refer you more often to more people. And, they'll willingly and cheerfully do that on your behalf, because you've already created the relational groundwork for that to happen.

Chapter 8

Install Your Customer Boomerang to Keep Them Coming Back.

You've most likely heard a version of this in the past, that there's more wealth in the customers you've already got than there is in the constant chase and expense for more new customers.

But what you might not have heard is that if you do it the proper way, marketing and making offers to your existing customers doesn't actually cost you a penny more in new advertising costs.

I don't know what the accurate figure is currently but we've all heard the different claims that it's maybe 5, 6, or even 7 times more expensive to acquire a brand new Customer than it is to get an existing happy customer to order or visit again. And even though this now seems obvious, it bears reinforcing that the bulk of the money you'll make is due to this one single business truism: THE MONEY IS IN THE FOLLOW UP.

And yet, even though it's true that there's plenty of money left on the table by not having any follow up process, by sending a constant set of ongoing communications to customers who have already had a wonderful experience with your business, could, if they're treated well and with kindness and respect, they could become some of your best and loyal customers. But that can never happen if you don't follow up. If you never keep in regular and constant touch. If you never acknowledge or appreciate them.

But importantly, what actually stops a business from following up and keeping in touch with their customers?

There are a few core reasons and when you see them, it may make uncomfortable reading. But strangely, that might be a good thing because if by reading them they in turn get you to take the necessary actions to change things around, you'll find you'll have created an ongoing income stream within your business that'll not only ramp up your profits on a consistent basis because of your customers returning again and again, but it'll have a happy and positive impact on your entire business and life.

Core Reasons:

1. Not enough time to follow up
2. Don't know how to create follow up communications
3. Don't know how to structure effective offers
4. Too busy doing other things in the business
5. To stressed or too lazy to find out
6. Technology is too overwhelming to figure out
7. The costs are too high to keep on following up
8. Staff somehow convince the owner that it's dangerous trying something new

In talking to and working with many pubs, restaurants, takeaways and coffee shops, we found through our research that nearly all operated with some kind of limiting belief or assumption about the follow up process, with many of those beliefs and assumptions rooted in the core reasons mentioned above.

Those limiting beliefs and assumptions are costing tens of thousands of small business operators everywhere from making really good money in a consistent, predictable and reliable way.

Looked at another way, most restaurants, takeaways, pubs and coffee shops are literally stealing from themselves in broad daylight, each and every day because of not having a follow up boomerang process and system operating in their businesses. When all it takes is to have their current and existing customers communicated to and contacted in a streamlined, simple and effortless way.

In fact, in a short while, I'll show you how incredibly simple and how unbelievably cheap and cost effective it is to have your own customer boomerang follow up system working for you and bringing in business for you as regularly, reliably and dependably as a Swiss Watch. 9

Chapter 9

Do You Know What Your Customer Lifetime Value Is?

Most in business, and this is from my experience of having worked with and helped hundreds of pubs and restaurant owners, managers and marketing teams, is that most do not know what their average customer is worth to them in profit terms, over the life of their customer.

And the reason for that is because most tend to look at a customer as a one-time transaction in their business, only looking at today's income, only asking...how can I make money, today?

But, almost never ever looking at their customer as a long-term residual asset who'll continue to supply the business with their patronage and their money for as long as they remain a happy and satisfied customer.

So why is knowing the lifetime value of your customer an important thing to know for you? And, what can you do with that information?

Well, let's look at how to actually calculate what that figure could be for you, and then, we can see what we can do once we've got that number.

Let's say that the following is true.

31

And follow along with this example as a guideline. Your numbers could be more, or less. That's not the main thing just now. What is the main thing, is following the formula and then if you like, you can put your own numbers in, which is what I suggest you do because then you will have a clear and accurate understanding of how to plot and plan your next move armed with this valuable information.

So, let's just say that the following is true for you, for one of your customers, where their average life with you as a customer is 4 years –

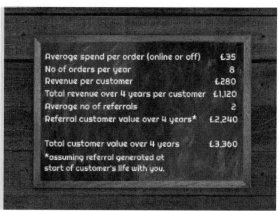

Average spend per order (online or off)	£35
No of orders per year	8
Revenue per customer	£280
Total revenue over 4 years per customer	£1,120
Average no of referrals	2
Referral customer value over 4 years*	£2,240
Total customer value over 4 years	£3,360

*assuming referral generated at start of customer's life with you.

So, based on the above figures, which as you can see has deliberately been put on the low side, each client that comes through your door or through the Internet as a new customer, is potentially worth £3360 to you over a 4 year period.

What that should tell you is that even if you were to invest £100, £200, £300, even £1000 just to get one customer, that single customer will still be worth a couple of thousand pounds to you over their admittedly short life tenure with you, as per our example.

And what that should also tell you is that each time you, lose a customer, and depending during what time frame they go, they're walking out with a future bank amount of money that again, runs into the thousands.

Now here's the brain troubling part; Multiply that lost customer number by 10 or 20 each year, you can see that those numbers quickly add up to huge chunks of lost cash down the road. Which quite conceivably, could be the monetary equivalent of having you take care of multiple monthly mortgage payments, could be the equivalent of getting yourself and your family a much needed exotic holiday each year for multiple years, or it could be the equivalent of having you put enough money down on a deposit for your kids home, or their university fees, or any number of other high cost payments.

That's the seriousness of knowing what your numbers are, and, doing all that you can do to protect them.

So, work out your customer lifetime value. Then find delightful ways to increase their total patronage time with you. Increase their frequency of purchases per year. Develop ways to increase the average order amount. Do those few little things and you'll have a business that's not just based on how you're doing week to week, but, instead, you'll be building an Equity based business that you can in the future, sell for big numbers.

But only if you consistently focus on turning your customers into lifetime valuable assets.

The good thing is you're about to find out how you can do that in a simple way that'll quite literally astound you as to both how simple it is, and yet at the same time, how dynamic and how wonderfully profitable it will be for you. No Neurofen required.

Chapter 10

Beware of the Technology and Marketing Minefields

How can you win the new online restaurant battle for customers and profits if opening your inbox each day is like opening up a new marketing bomb? One that'll instantly detonate inside your head, causing you infinitely more chaos and confusion that's most likely adding to your existing levels of chaos and confusion?

Frankly, you can't listen to everyone, and you cannot buy every single marketing and advertising method out there, or invest in every single automation system being promoted, or scooping up each bit of new marketing technology that comes out. You can't be doing more things that'll add to the chaos and confusion.

And yet, what I should more accurately say and convey is the available tools and technology that are out there all probably work to some level. Yet the core issue is about knowing what to employ and use, and, knowing and understanding how it all integrates together to form a reliable, marketing and customer generating system that brings you back more than you invest in it.

So that's what you want to be focusing on and figuring out because once you get the right marketing and technology formula working for your restaurant, takeaway, pub or coffee shop, not only will you be able to save yourself a huge amount of time, money, energy and frustration, but you'll be able to create a level of business certainty and security that's based on science, formula and accurate data and information.

In other words, it's a process that's built on rock and not on sand.

So how do you know what are the right marketing and technology ingredients for your specific venue? How do you know what are your best tools and processes you should be using? How do you know whether you should be using Google Ads, Facebook, blog marketing, leaflet drops, articles, video marketing, LinkedIn, local newspaper advertising, event marketing, text message marketing? How do you know what's the best and optimal way to integrate everything together in order to have your customer generating marketing system working seamlessly for you?

The only way you'll know what's the perfect formula for you and for you to not step on multiple minefields every place you turn, is to see what's currently working for others and adopt and model that system for your own venue.

And so how do you model what's currently working? And, how can you get into the nitty gritty details of what's working because a successful restaurant or takeaway, or pub or coffee shop isn't necessarily going to welcome you with open arms and sit you down to show you how things are done around there and give you the formula blueprint and the tools to copy and emulate what's currently working there for them. They're unlikely to do that.

However, the good news for you is because we've been working with many restaurant, takeaways, pubs and coffee shops over the years, and especially now, in this new economic world we're living in, we've seen at close quarters what's currently working for them and the specific tools and methods employed to help simplify the process, eradicate almost all chaos and confusion and, to give them a level of confidence and certainty they didn't possess when the entire world almost came to an economic halt, with the hospitality and restaurants trades being one of those hit the hardest.

In the next chapter, you'll be shown how you can win the new online restaurant battle for customers and profits, without you having to step on any marketing landmines and without you having your brains filled with endless amounts of chaos and confusion.

Chapter 11

Whose Brand Are You Building Anyway?

Admittedly it seems an utterly bizarre question but how can you profitably sell a business having no customers that you actually own? (And by actually own, I mean owning their customer data and information)

To help you answer that question, when you originally launched your business you most likely decided on the colour scheme, the logo, your brand name, how you wanted your website to look, the graphics, all of that.

And naturally, you most likely thought that selling to customers automatically meant that you owned that customer information, which you could use in any way you liked in the future to create whatever marketing communications you wanted to. That just seems a normal and natural conclusion to make. It's how we all think and believe.

And yet, believe it or not, you can have a business where you sell your takeaways or restaurant take outs, where you own almost none of the customers you sell to. But how can that be? How exactly does that process work?

It works by you paying for the privilege having a third party online App ordering and online based delivery business acting on your behalf, getting you customers through their marketing and advertising efforts, and yet, it's where you pay for each time a customer places an order, no matter how often they buy from you through that third-party vendor.

And so guess who is building that third party Brand? And at the same time, guess who is having their own brand diluted and weakened? It's plain and simple. It's those restaurant owners, takeaway businesses, and food places, who are having their own brand diluted, and, who are paying for the third party online App businesses to elevate their own brands. Brands like Just Eat and Deliveroo.

So how do you build your own brand without giving a lot of commission away to 3rd party businesses and without losing any customer information and contact data.? Whilst at the same time, taking advantage of the new available technology. And also taking advantage of the most important factor of all – the heightened daily dependency and usage of their mobile phones – so how do you build your own brand through all of that that has value, equity, endless star appeal?

I'm going to reveal it to you and I encourage you to read through the following chapters because you'll soon see how you can win the New Restaurant Online Battle for Customers & Profits.

Chapter 12

'

Birthday & Anniversary Marketing:

Your Untapped Profit Centre – Celebrating Special Events

There's nothing sweeter for a person than celebrating their birthday, anniversary or other special yearly event, and celebrating that event with friends and family. (Of course, there's a small number who simply dislike the whole celebratory thing so naturally, this isn't targeted to them!)

What's rare however, is for that person to receive a special invitation, special recognition of that celebratory event from a business, from *any* business. Sadly, for the customers, there are very few businesses making a big hoopla over a person's birthday or their special event.

In fact, unless they've kept records because of having asked for that specific information in some way, most businesses don't even know their customers birthdays, anniversaries, or special occasions. And whether they do know it or not, probably only one in a thousand businesses, if that, really cares beyond sending out the regulatory *'Happy Birthday'* email. But even that's stretching it.

And yet, for restaurants, pubs, takeaway, coffee shops, that piece of news should be music to your ears because generally, what's the one thing people mostly do on their special occasion? That's right… they eat! And in many cases, they eat a lot, and that too, with friends and family.

And what's also true is that eating and celebrating is not only reserved for dinner time, it can happen any time of day. And if it's a 'really big number event', the occasion could run over a few days.

But still, even if that's feels like wonderful news to you, I need to report that unless you know the special event dates in your customers lives, your venue will simply be one of many on the spinning roulette wheel in your customers mind when it comes to *what* and *where* they'll eat on their birthday, anniversary or special occasion.

Hoping, wishing and praying they choose you, where they show up or order from your venue, as the happy by-product of luck and chance, is no way to ensure you're the obvious choice venue.

And in case you didn't know the money numbers as to what happens if you had a few additional birthday events celebrated or food being ordered through your venue, you'll be both delightfully amazed and devastatingly *sickened* at the same time.

Amazed and incredulous at exactly how much additional money you could be generating each week, month and year in your venue through a formalised and systematised birthday and event marketing process (and also, amazed at how ridiculously simple and easy it is to put in place – see the Facebook chapter as being one possibility) …

… and also, devastatingly sickened at the bulk of money you've lost in the past by not having a formalised birthday and event marketing process in your venue, and also… **the bulk of future money you'll soon lose** by not doing anything different about what you now know about birthday and event marketing.

The Numbers

Because of not knowing what your specific numbers are in your venue in terms of the number of customers you have, the various prices you sell at, the amount you put aside to generate business, etc, let's say that you had one new additional birthday event being celebrated at your venue each week. And, that the party, or order, was for 8 people. And let's say that it's a £30 per person amount.

That's £240 in business. Add in another £100 for drinks and dessert, that's £340. (What's not being deducted here is the cost of overhead or what it cost to produce the food. You'll have to factor in that contribution.)

So that's £340 in new business each week. On a yearly basis, that's £17,680 (52 x £340)

Now if just one of those people who were celebrating in each of those celebratory groups each week, also had their special event at your venue sometime in the year, that's another 52 additional birthdays or celebrations going on in the year, bringing in the same £17,680 in new business.

And of course, as a happy by-product of you serving your customers extraordinary well, there'll obviously be uncounted for residual and referral business coming your way that will add and compound to the healthy cash flow and income stability of your venue.

Ask yourself, would you like an additional £35k+ in business each year, just by knowing what the dates of those special events are in your customers lives are; and then knowing how to send out a few simple communications that'll have your customers delighted to want you to provide the food for their special occasion, again and again and again?

You know this for a fact; your customers are going to celebrate their birthdays. Anniversaries, and other special occasions somewhere, with people, with money, with food, so you might as well orchestrate it in a way that your venue is on the top of their list, each and every time.

Celebrating birthdays and events is a nice fat profit centre, yet most venues treat it as being something that's left to chance. You don't want to leave anything to chance, especially in today's turbulent and unpredictable economic climate.

Chapter 13

Help, How Can I Get Facebook to Work for Me?

A high number of pubs, restaurants and other food-based business owners have said to me they've tried Facebook advertising but it doesn't work for them.

And yet, when I dig a little deeper, I find owners have got the wrong information from the gaggle of Facebook Ad practitioners who talk a great talk, are even better at taking money. And yet, when it comes down to producing results and bringing in paying customers for pennies per click, they've a look on their face like they've been asked to write a letter in ancient Egyptian hieroglyphics.

Others try a little of this and a little of that, never ever really understanding the driving principles behind how to make Facebook work for them.

Facts are, to get any kind of quality result there are specific fundamentals and rules to learn, follow and then implement. Most don't follow and implement because they have a low tolerance and impatience threshold for learning the core fundamentals.

Instead, they want shortcuts, hacks, quick fixes, money saving tricks to try to '*game*' the system. And yes, they want them fast.

So when they play around with Facebook (that's the correct term because many are simply playing around and not taking it as a serious marketing and profit generating tool) ...when they don't get immediate results, they abandon the whole effort and put it down to the ineffectiveness of the marketing tool and process, and never ever think about turning the finger of blame inwards.

The Good News?

Here are 5 pieces of exciting information about Facebook that'll help you leverage its incredible power and how it can be a blockbuster catalyst for you in your pub, restaurant or food-based venue.

1. Facebook recently launched something called 'Facebook ad library' which means you can now research what your competitors are doing on Facebook in an open and transparent way.

   In fact the ad library provides a comprehensive view of all ads running on Facebook and when you consider the importance of research when running a business, this is truly amazing, and available to everyone to see and use.

2. Facebook's Retargeting tool will follow those prospects who clicked your ads and will show up as an omni-present, non-stalker like, silent Internet visual sales person, wherever they go online. That little retargeting ad will act like it's your prospects constant memory system and it'll only be a matter of time where they'll decide to click the ads and follow the call to action you've created.

   The results of this stealth like follow-up system, is huge. You could recoup a good proportion of your ad costs on those prospects, prospects whom you most likely thought were long gone out of your life. And yet, without the retargeting element working for you, you'll never know how much money you could be losing.

3. The appetite for video and watching video on the internet, is sky rocketing. And, it's not going to stop anytime soon. And if you want proof and evidence of this fact, simply pull up the stats for YouTube video watching and you'll see how this Internet video watching trend is simply not going to go away.

    What that means for you is simple video based ads for your restaurant or venue will get watched, responded to and bought from through Facebook. More importantly, video ads are not at all complicated to set up and launch.

4. By uploading your customer's email and SMS information into the Facebook ad platform, Facebook will automatically allow you to send targeted ads to that data that they recognise and that matches up with their systems, thus helping you create the best targeted message that's sent to the most likely set of people who will respond.

    Not only will you now eradicate all the marketing and advertising waste by NOT advertising to those people who aren't right fit or match, but, you'll now be able to advertise to ONLY those people and prospects who are most likely to respond and buy from you.

5. You do not have to commit any kind of major ad spend or budget to test the validity of your ads and campaigns. Believe it or not, you can spend as little £5 or £10 a day if you wish. Testing various ads on a small budget and seeing what works and what doesn't, allows you to scale and ramp up what does work, and, throw away and abandon what doesn't work before committing any kind of higher investment.

    Never before has any other media allowed you to carry out such tests and experiments and that too, at such a low investment cost. Normally, if you wanted to test the market with various promotional offers, you'd at least have to invest the minimum when launching a campaign – whether newspaper ads, tv, direct mail, radio, event marketing, and, you can't pause the whole effort and make tweaks and changes half way through. And that minimum investment would easily set you back hundreds, if not thousands of pounds.

With Facebook advertising working for you, you'll be able to track to the penny what's working and what's not, what's cost effective and what has to be abandoned. And, you can   start employing this incredible medium, quickly. There's no stalling, waiting or endless hoops you have to jump through. And best of all, penny for penny, pound for pound, it's the most cost effective media you can use to bring a customer in.

Let's take a look at how "Facebook Targeting" works:

When anyone opens a Facebook account, people can, as an option, provide their date of birth and wedding anniversary date as well.

What this means for you is **you can target only those local people who have a birthday or anniversary** and target them with a laser focused, compelling offer to book a table, or order an online celebration takeaway.

Here's some recent Facebook campaign insights:

1. Target within a 6 mile radius
2. In the next 60 days
3. 28,000 targeted individuals with Birthdays
4. 8,000 targeted individuals with Wedding Anniversaries
5. Age Band 18 to 65 yrs old
6. Works for Dine In or Takeaway

7. Collection or Takeaway
8. Special Pre-order Celebration offer
9. Target friends of people with birthdays

What most owners don't know, and that's because of being fed the wrong information or they've made general sweeping (wrong) assumptions, is that through Facebook, by small low cost marketing tests, it can result in huge wins, if you know what you're doing.

This really is, for now, a huge untapped area for you as an owner and must focus a proportion of your time on because it's currently the most cost effective marketing strategy there is, or ever has been.

Frankly, there isn't anything quite like it for an owner to turn their business into a filled-to-capacity business, whilst spending comparatively little to nothing to bring business in compared to the many other ultra expensive marketing media options that are available.

And, when Facebook is used in conjunction with your own App for your venue, you'll possess and own a powerful and profitable marketing and technology combination that'll ensure your business thrives and prospers, no matter what kind of economy we're in.

Chapter14

Your Winning Restaurant Strategy

The One Single Tool That'll Revolutionise the Way You Do Business in Your Restaurant, Pub, Takeaway or Coffee Shop… but Only If You Want to Win the Online Battle for Customers and Profits

You may have now figured out that the way to create advantage, distinction and win the New Restaurant online game, is to have your own prestigiously branded App.

An App will not only allow you get more customers, make more and more sales, and do it in a consistent, reliable and dependable way, but it will also allow you to command the kind of professional respect and marketplace positioning normally reserved in the past for businesses with deep pockets, oodles of influence and lots of star appeal.

You can now be part of that group, yet without needing any of the above past pre-requisites.

Now think about this scenario:

Your business is now closed for the evening. The place is all tidied up and you make your way back home, albeit rather pooped and exhausted. You say hi to the family or those I your home of flat, grab something to eat, (something from your own venue of course!") maybe grab a little tv or surf the Internet then it's time to go over the days numbers and plan for tomorrow.

Some days you wish it'd be over in the blink of an eye. And then, it's now lights out. You're happy for 40 winks of un-interrupted shut eye.

And yet, unbeknownst to you, whist you were sleeping, a certain number of your customers who have previously downloaded your prestigious App onto their smart phone, are up into the wee small hours, many of them planning their days and nights a few days ahead at a time. And, they're actually on your venue's App, making an order for food for a time in the future – tomorrow, the day after, or the day after.

Yes, you're receiving pre-orders even when your business is closed and when you're grabbing 40 winks!

Pie in the sky thinking? Could have been, in the past. Not now. It's a new reality.

Now for many, that's the ultimate business scenario, not doing any kind of heavy extensive marketing except letting people know about your App for your venue, which your customers can download anytime of day or night they want, where they can place an order from your menus' through your App, any time of day and night.

And the good thing is that by making a pre-order, they've ALREADY paid you for that order, just like you'd pre-order a book on Amazon, except, they're doing this not by phoning up or sending an email, they're selecting, clicking and paying through your own personal App.

Now it can't get better than that, can it?

Well, it can, because your own personalised business App acts like the very best marketing team you can ever employ for pennies on the pound.

Yet unlike human beings, your App works ceaselessly and tirelessly for you, never sleeps, never calls in sick, never mistreats your customers, can help you generate new daily business, makes referrals for you on your behalf, helps you deliver special celebrations communications and offers, tracks all customer spend down to the penny, even lets YOU be the celebrity on your App to your customers!

Frankly, there's never been such a technological, marketing and automation revolution like there is with owning and having your own prestigious App for your business.

An App built and customised for you from the ground up. And amazingly, it's where you can almost run your entire business right from the palm of your hand.

And here's first hand proof of that:

I was deflated and miserable, in two minds what to do. Business was down. Since working with Neil our results have been great. I'm more calm, happier and more certain that Coronavirus or not, we're going to be doing well because of the help, the marketing strategies and the personal guidance from Neil and his team.

Tito Fernandez

Owner Mumbai Brasserie & Andover Tandoori

App downloads = 737
On-line orders = 428
Pre-orders = £31
Customer spend = £15,985
Savings on Just Eat commissions = £2238
Savings on Just Eat transaction fees = £214

Total savings on Just Eat = £2452

Most of all building the Mumbai Brasserie brand

App Downloads

And for those restaurants, pubs, takeaways, coffee shops and other food based businesses who are looking for that key advantage that'll help them rise above the rest of their competitive marketplace, especially in this most crippling of economic times, then the seemingly obvious solution will be to invest in an App for their food based business.

But of course, even the seemingly obvious isn't adhered to or followed and so that's why **here are 10 reasons why an App could be the best investment you could make in your business,** especially if you are unhappy and dissatisfied with the current economic scenario and how uncertain you feel about what's going to happen regarding your future.

1. An App is fully compliant with government advice and guidance. And that's been the case because of the encouraging of social distancing rules, contactless table side ordering, and less human contact.

2. An App system provides a real sense of stability, certainty, and predictability in your business. It also gives your customers and staff a level of confidence and peace of mind due to the controlled order and systematised nature an App brings into your business.

3. You've a complete and easy-to-see record of how many customers have ordered a takeaway or visited your restaurant,. You'll get to know exactly who they are and you won't have this important data hidden from you as you would if you were to have a third party business controlling things with their App system.

4. You can now easily follow-up and send promotions from the palm of your hand to your customer who have downloaded your App and so you can do away with all the messy complicated methods you employed in the past with sending follow up promotions and special offers.

5. Online Orders for takeaway, table booking online or Contactless table-side ordering is safe, fast, secure and easy.

6. An App put you squarely inside the place the where your customers spend a high percentage of their time, on their mobile phones. And when you consider most online purchases are made via a phone compared to purchasing on a laptop or pc, you're inside their preferred buying habit and you'll be in sync with them by a using a process your customers are currently already using and are used to.

7. Your customers can easily download the App via a variety of ways. For example - from your website, via a QR Code, by informing them via a link in an email, putting a simple instructional message on your takeaway bags, or your food receipts, on a simple leaflet, a tasteful message on your front door.

8. An App easily integrates with your overall marketing efforts and can easily help connect the various dots, whether you choose both online and offline media as part of your marketing mix. And it's quite possible that you will soon find that you'll do away with the majority of your marketing media you currently use as compared to the App, they're not as cost effective as you thought they were.

9. Setting up and installing the core components of an App, are straightforward to set up – the online orders, pre-orders, he payment system, table booking, contactless table-side ordering.

10. The affordability of a prestigious marketing tool working for you in your business is no more expensive than most monthly phone bills, yet for your business, the rewards and returns could quite easily dwarf the minimal investment, and yet, you need to be fully aware whom you decide to engage in an App project for your business because you can quite easily be taken for a ride by a smooth talking money-grabber, quoting you anything from £10k to £75k+ for your own functional App.

With your own prestigious App working for you in your business, the advantages to you are many:

You get to own your own media. You get to call the shots. You get to make all the money. You get to build an asset. You get to keep all your customer info and data. You don't need to pay third-party fees for each customer transaction. You get the certainty and relief of enjoying and running your business, all over again. And, most important of all, no matter what the economy is doing, no matter what your competitors or marketplace is doing, you'll be able to keep on creating business and profits and your App will help you keep the connection and relationship with your customers running smoothly, profitably and continuously.

In fact it's reported by TechCrunch that the coronavirus impact has sent app downloads, usage and consumer spending to record highs in Q2 of 2020.

According to new data from App Store intelligence firm app Annie, mobile app usage grew 40% year-over-year in the second quarter of 2020 even hitting an all time high of over 200 billion hours in April 2020.

Consumer spending in apps meanwhile hit an all time high $27 billion dollars in the second quarter and consumers downloaded 35 billion new apps being an all time high.

Zoom for instance became the no 2 of most downloaded app globally in Q2 and Google meet was no 7 just proving it really is an app world.

The second quarter of 2020 was the biggest yet for mobile apps – downloads, usage, and, yes, spending. During the time, mobile app usage shot up 40% hitting an all-time high of over 20 billion hours during April.

And as for spending:

Consumer spending in apps, meanwhile, hit a record high of $27 billion in the second quarter. And app downloads reached a high of nearly 35 billion.

Don't think this trend is reversing any time soon. It's just warming up. The trends, numbers, and sales have been pointing towards mobile over desktop for a long time

Conclusion

Please Don't Just Sit There and Do Nothing

Thank you for reading to the end of this book.

Now what you've read in this publication can serve you in one of two ways.

The first way this publication can serve you is as a glaring and startling reminder, to dramatically highlight what's currently going on in your in venue, in your industry, in your geographic locality. And, that the local retail and commerce environment has changed, dramatically.

But even though that's the case, you find yourself unsure, unwilling, uncommitted to want to do anything more than absorb what you've read, then file the information away in your mind for another time - where you *might* bring the information out because either you're seeing that you need to be doing something differently... or...maybe sometime in the future you'll dust off the covers of this publication and really take it to heart because your situation has then become even worse and more uncertain than you thought.

The other way this publication can serve you is by having it prodded, pinched, provoked you into the new dramatic realisation that if you just sit there and do nothing different than what you're currently doing, then you can emotionally feel it inside and where you look down the road a little that your gut tells you that this whole scenario is not going to end well for you, your venture, your livelihood.

And, because of that scary realisation, you've found that what you've read has now pushed and compelled you to rethink, re-evaluate and re-strategise either some, part or your *entire* modus operandi.

If that's the case, please listen to this very important piece of news:

You do NOT need to accept what's going on in the economy. You do NOT need to listen to the voices of woe and timidity whom you're most likely surrounded by -- at home, in the media, in listening to the many gloom filled restaurant owners, pubs owners, coffee shops and takeaways owners. You don't need to buy into any of their stories at all.

Instead, you want to model and emulate the way a small minority of Owners and how they're doing everything right, who are passionate and excited about the new opportunity that's presented to them, who are thrilled and excited about the fact that because the majority of their competitors are running blind with a stack of inaccurate beliefs, depressingly bad amounts information, woefully poor advice, suffering with a high dose of internally driven fear and confusion...

... and because of their competitors not doing anything differently, these small handful of successful Owners will get to clean up and dominate their geographic marketplace, all happening by default because the majority aren't willing to do anything different.

And that strange and profitably cosy situation is available to you also, if you decide to take to heart what you've found in this publication and make the necessary changes you have to be making if you want to thrive and prosper... and NOT act like the majority who are locked into panic and long term finger pointing and blaming which'll quickly accelerate the rate at which they will either close down completely, or whimper to an almost complete stand still, frozen with inaction.

Your Special Bonus:

As a special bonus for reading to the end of this publication, if you are an owner who is at the same time both excited yet unsure about what your next move should be, then you're invited to a special restaurant online web-seminar called "How to not be a Dinosaur Restaurant" ...it's all about how to not get left behind and make your local competition irrelevant, just go to

www.nodinosaurrestaurants.com

and register.

BITE-SIZED
BOOKS

Bite-Sized Business Books are designed to provide support and insights for professionals who are tackling an unfamiliar task either for the first time or after a gap, as well as those who want to find new ways of doing what they are familiar with.

They are deliberately short, easy to read, step-by-step manuals and books guiding the reader through the various stages behind each business process or activity, with a clear focus on outcomes. They are firmly based on personal experience and success.

The most successful people all share an ability to focus on what really matters, keeping things simple and understandable. MBAs, metrics and methodologies have their place, but when we are faced with a new challenge most of us need quick guidance on what matters most, from people who have been there before and who can show us where to start. As Stephen Covey famously said, "The main thing is to keep the main thing, the main thing".

But what exactly is the main thing?

Bite-Sized books were conceived to help answer precisely that question crisply and fast and, of course, be engaging to read, written by people who are experienced and successful in their field.

The brief? Distil the "main things" into a book that can be read by an intelligent non-expert comfortably in around 60 minutes.

Make sure the book enables the reader with specific tools, ideas and plenty of examples drawn from real life and business. Be a virtual mentor.

Bite-Sized Books don't cover every eventuality, but they are written from the heart by successful people who are happy to share their experience with you and give you the benefit of their success.

We have avoided jargon – or explained it where we have used it as a shorthand – and made few assumptions about the reader, except that they are in business, are literate and numerate, and that they can adapt and use what we suggest to suit their own, individual purposes. Whether you are working for a multi-national corporation or a start-up or something in between, the principles we introduce will hold good.

They can be read straight through at one easy sitting and then used as a support while you are working on what you need to do.

Bite-Sized Books Catalogue

We publish Business Books, Life-Style Books, Public Affairs Books, including our Brexit Books, Fiction – both short form and long form – and Children's Fiction.

To see our full range of books, please go to https://bite-sizedbooks.com/.

Printed in Great Britain
by Amazon